ANGELS
AND OTHER
BEINGS OF LIGHT

THEY ARE HERE TO HELP YOU!

A Discourse from the Ascended Master

ST. GERMAIN

Linda Stein-Lu
Martin F. Luthke,

Expansion Publishing

ANGELS AND OTHER BEINGS OF LIGHT

THEY ARE HERE TO HELP YOU!

A Discourse from the Ascended Master
ST. GERMAIN

Linda Stein-Luthke
Martin F. Luthke, Ph.D.

Copyright © 1998 by Linda Stein-Luthke & Martin F. Luthke

Third printing: September 2005

ISBN 0-9656927-3-6

Expansion Publishing
P.O. Box 516 - Chagrin Falls, OH 44022
USA

Contents

Foreword

It is with great joy that we offer this third book in a series of publications inspired by the Ascended Master St. Germain. We would not have chosen to be part of this collaboration had we not experienced what we describe in this book. We agreed to work with St. Germain once again to let you know that it is possible for anyone to experience what we write about.

Even as we moved through the process of editing and publishing what St. Germain had offered to us, we felt the continuous presence of these blessed beings of Light.

As an illustration we would like to share one particular incident with you. When we were approaching the deadline for the printing of this book, which had to be available in time for an important speaking engagement, we suddenly realized that the manuscript had too many pages for the printing format we had anticipated. As a consequence, the book would be more expensive and time consuming to produce. This was unwelcome news because we felt we neither had time nor money to spare!

After receiving this news, at the end of a long day, Linda went to bed. In her mind she debated whether we should reduce the length of the manuscript, which could have solved what appeared to be a significant "problem."

Long into the night Martin continued working on the manuscript. The next morning, when Linda arose after a short and restless night, she found paperwork as well as the computer that now contained the manuscript by the window in the kitchen. This window is adorned with several angel figures that had been given to us over the years. One of the most beautiful angels had fallen off the window and was now resting on top of the paperwork on the table. This particular angel figure had been securely stuck to the window pane since we first received it. It had never "traveled" before. From time to time other objects symbolizing the Light had moved about our house as a way of catching our attention, but never this one.

Linda stopped to listen within and asked herself why this would have happened. Instantly, she felt comforted and realized that there was no reason to be concerned. The work had been blessed from the beginning, as have all of our endeavors. No text would have to be omitted. The book was in perfect order -- and so was the process of publishing it.

This loving reminder by our invisible friends helped her to relax, to let go of her fears, and to allow trust to return. It is but one small example of how Angels and other Beings of Light enrich and bless our lives.

Another example is the existence of this book, which developed in collaboration between beings who reside on different planes. For some, it may be more than a stretch to accept the reality of invisible Beings of Light in general, and Ascended Masters in particular. We can only appeal to your willingness to suspend your disbelief and to entertain, and test, the teachings offered on these pages. Countless perfectly "normal" and "sane" human beings have already opened themselves to an awareness of the reality of Beings of Light, and have benefited immeasurably in the process. You, too, may be greatly enriched by opening your heart and mind to the Light.

Most importantly, however, we encourage you to listen to your own "still small voice within" and to the guidance you will be receiving, if only you choose to sit, meditate, and ask. We offer our truth as a service, but, above all, we wish you to honor your own truth! And now, enjoy the journey within.

Love and Light,

September, 1998   Linda & Martin

ABOUT THE AUTHORS

We have found that it is generally easier to relate to new information if you have at least a vague idea of the person or source it is coming from. Thus, before we get to the main topic of this book, let us take a minute to introduce ourselves.

St. Germain is one of the Ascended Masters, a group of Beings of Light who once walked this Earth in human bodies and who have gained complete awareness of their Totality. They are serving humanity and all of Creation from the higher planes of existence, offering their Light, Love, and Wisdom freely to all at this auspicious time of accelerating change. St. Germain is the source of inspiration behind this publication and its true author.

Linda Stein-Luthke is the one who brought the following text to paper. Among her many gifts is the ability to "channel" wisdom from sources other than her human consciousness. Channeling is a process during which we open ourselves to higher vibrational frequencies of Light. The frequencies we access can be from our own being or from other beings of Light working in conjunction with us. For many years Linda, or "Leia," as she is called by the Masters, has been channeling highly evolved spiritual beings of Light, most frequently the Ascended Masters El Morya

3

Khan and St. Germain as well as the Light of the Christos and the Ma (i.e., Divine Mother) energy.

Linda has been a practitioner and teacher of astrology for more than twenty-five years. In addition, she works as a metaphysical teacher, healer and medical intuitive, using the various skills she has learned during her many years "on the path" and learning new ones every step of the way. She has been a mother and foster mother, successful business woman, activist and philanthropist in the women's community, and, first and foremost, a seeker throughout her life. She has traveled widely and has collaborated with masters from various parts of the world. Her training has been within the Hindu, Buddhist, Sufi, Christian, and Jewish faiths. Linda has been a presenter at national and international conferences, as well as a leader of workshops and trainings.

Dr. Martin Luthke is a clinical psychologist with in-depth training in traditional psychology and psychotherapy. His current practice, however, has shifted entirely to an energy-based paradigm. Together with his wife Linda, he has developed an advanced energy-psychological approach called Psychoenergetic Healing. Martin is the founder and director of the *Institute of Psychoenergetic Healing* and the (co-)author of several books and publications. He is a healer and metaphysical teacher, and has given workshops, trainings and presentations in the United States and Europe. Martin took responsibility for the editing and production aspects of this collaborative project. (We thank Julianne Stein for her invaluable contributions in the editing process.)

Together, Martin and Linda are parenting two grown children, two elementary school children, three cats, and a dog.

Introduction

Beloved children, we thank you, once again, for allowing us this opportunity to come to you to write, through this one called "Leia," of very important matters. Very important matters, indeed. For you see, beloved ones, as your Earth plane is rapidly increasing in frequency, many of you are beginning to experience phenomena that you find difficult to assimilate and comprehend. Others may not as yet have begun to experience these phenomena, but rest assured, all that are open will eventually know of these things whether they consciously choose such an awareness or not.

We say "consciously choose such an awareness," for all who are alive now have *chosen* to be here to experience this time of great awakening for the whole Earth plane. If a phenomenal experience comes to you during this time of awakening, and you did not know consciously that you wished this experience, we assure you that on some level of awareness, you did express such a desire. In time you will comprehend such matters more easily. Certainly, the more you allow yourself to experience these phenomena, the easier such a comprehension will be.

So, it is time, dear ones, to tell you of these things, so that you can learn what to do when such phenomena occur. Now, you may choose to call these phenomena "Angels and other beings of Light." It is a very good name, and one that many humans can comprehend easily. What happens, however, for some is that various thought forms become attached to these labels. This we wish to help you with at this time, for these thought forms may give rise to some questions.

5

One of these questions may be: Do we exist, we, who are writing this book and are called Ascended Masters?[1] You may then, of course, also ask if Angels exist. And if so, what are they and where have they come from? Further, you might ask: Why would they help us? Am I, as a human, worthy of their help? Then you may also ask: How may I see an Angel or being of Light and how can I believe what I see? And there may be many other questions that we have not as yet addressed. You see, as soon as anything is given a label in your world, there are thought forms attached to it and questions that arise with the thought forms.

Now, in response to these questions, would you believe us if we were to tell you that the Light in all its forms, whether as Angels or other forms, has always been with you to aid you and love you continuously since the beginning of all time and space? Would you also believe that somewhere within your own being you have always known this, and on some level have been continuously connected with the Light whether you were consciously aware of this or not?

Possibly, just possibly you might believe this. And we will tell you that **this is all true**. Then, if we were to tell you that these Angels and beings of Light have become a reality in order to facilitate your awareness of the Light within, would you believe this? Furthermore, we will say that you have, as humans, co-created the reality of these beings to aid yourselves in an awareness of this Light. For the Light itself is benevolent and loving, and in its service to you has helped you co-create all that you experience. We will then tell you that **all these things are true**.

---

[1] In this context we are among the "other beings of Light."

6

So, we have given you much to think about right here at the beginning. And that is our purpose in the production of this writing: To bring thoughts to your awareness that may provoke in you a desire to learn more for yourself about the phenomena that are increasingly becoming known to all of you as "Angels and other beings of Light."

We wish to add, before we begin to explain things further, that all the beings of Light that we will mention operate at higher vibrational frequencies than those of which you are normally aware on the Earth plane. Therefore, they are not subject to that which you would call "time and space." The notions of space and time were created by humans to aid them in measuring their experience of the Earth plane. Higher vibrational beings of Light can know their experience of existing without needing such Earth-bound creations. Therefore, they are available to come to you and all others who invoke them simultaneously. Isn't that a wondrous concept!

Chapter 1

What is the Light?

What is this thing we call the "Light" -- this thing we claim flows through your being whether you are choosing to be aware of such or not? The Light has been with all and everything since the beginning of creation as it is understood on the Earth plane at this time. Using the term "Light" is a way of describing that which flows through you but, indeed, defies description by the human mind. We have chosen to call it "Light" so that you can comprehend intellectually that something is indeed animating your form and giving it Life.

Some beings call this the "life force that God gives you." Some call it the "life force that Allah gives you." Some call it "the Buddha within." Some call it the *Atman*. Many different religions and philosophies have labeled it in various ways. It is the center around which all religions, sciences and philosophies evolve. For the sake of this publication, we shall call it the Light. We endeavor by this label to avoid creating further religious belief, and instead will simply describe something which does, indeed, exist.

The nature of this Light is that it is **benevolent, loving, compassionate, wise and omniscient**. It does not ask that its presence be felt and understood. It simply is. Some have called it the *Aum* or hum of creation. When it is honored and recognized, it responds with celebration that awareness has been accomplished. When humans do not choose to honor and recognize the wonder and beauty of what flows through them, it still continues to supply life and love unconditionally and universally. It never blesses some

8

and curses others. It does not even have the capability to do such. It simply continues to exist as the breath and love of all creation. It has given humans a beautiful Earth, which they themselves have co-created, in which to reside in free will.

Humans can choose to recognize the Light or ignore it. However, since all humans are inextricably connected to the Light, the natural urge is to try to awaken to an awareness of this wondrous thing that has co-created all that can be sensed in everything, everywhere. We say "co-created," for the Light, in its love, has bent to the free will of humanity and allowed its incomprehensible resources to be used to co-create all that can be experienced as the Earth plane. When one curses "God," one is really cursing that which humanity has co-created with the Light. When one surrenders to the awareness of this wondrous Light, what has been cursed can be transformed, transmuted and healed for all time and space.

Everything on Earth and indeed, in all creation, possesses a vibrational frequency. Your scientists know this. Every atom, the building block of your universe as you perceive it, is continuously vibrating to a certain frequency. Your scientists also know that the vibrational frequency of your planet as a whole is increasing at this time.

This means that it is now easier than ever for humans to become aware of alternative frequencies that have not easily been perceived before. For instance, you may see the table in front of you, and know that it, too, contains atoms that have a vibrational frequency. We will tell you that this table is composed of Light, as is all creation, and this is what makes the vibration occur. What you may be able to see more easily now than ever before, is the Light that makes the atoms move within the table. This is the same Light that animates your human form. It is naturally within you already. If it were not, you would not exist.

The Light of which we speak is everywhere and in everything. However, because it is of a higher vibrational frequency than can easily be observed with the five physical senses of the human body, it is not easily perceived and/or understood by most. For the sake of those who choose to recognize the Light, we will say it is composed of **vibration, sound** and a **visual component** that you can most easily perceive as Light. If one is choosing a meditative practice, this practice usually will facilitate the ability to perceive the Light. For some, however, a realization may come effortlessly. For instance, some may first become aware of the phenomenal nature of the Light in the dream state.

The *Light*, when perceived, will be luminescent in nature, and one may perceive various shadings of color including pure gold, white, violet, blue, green, yellow, rose, magenta, and many shadings in between.

One may also be capable of feeling the *vibration*, which may be perceived as a tingling sensation, a feeling of warmth or fullness or simply a sensation of lightheadedness, as if one has had a bit too much of a very fine wine!

Some experience the *sound* as a buzzing or ringing that may become louder or softer, depending on how open one is to the experience at that moment.

One may also perceive the Light as *Angels, Archangels,* or other *beings of Light.* There will, of course, be more about that later.

Each person will have his or her own unique experience of the Light, because each being's Light is based on the unique frequency which that being possesses. We wish to emphasize that **every being is unique**, and therefore will have his or her own unique experience of the Light. This is most important to remember. Each being, upon the Earth

10

plane and elsewhere in creation, has a unique frequency of Light which is that being's "signature."

Any experience that one chooses will affect that unique frequency. Thus, it is subject to change as one moves through one's life. So you see, you continue to alter and change the nature of the Light you carry, depending on how you choose to live your life.

We also ask you to be clear, beloved ones, in knowing that this Light is the Life force that flows through you while you reside in a body on Earth. This force stays with you when you leave the Earth. In other words, it is eternal, as is all creation, in one form or another. Your journey upon the Earth is designed to help you gain as full an awareness as possible of this Light, and to allow it to be your ally as you have this experience called "human life."

Such an awareness can be called an **awakening to the true nature of your reality**. Such an awakening is to be treasured above all other human accomplishment. That is why you have chosen a journey upon the Earth: To awaken to the true nature of all reality. And **the true nature of all reality is that Life is Light**.

Chapter 2

Am I Worthy of the Light?

This is the question that we hear most frequently from those upon the human plane. It is the question that one may not even be aware that one asks, and yet it will most often be the reason a human is suffering. Although every human already carries the Light, few are aware of this. Most simply assume the Light would not find them worthy. Even the ones who know that they already possess the Light will still question their worthiness.

In the human consciousness, there are as many reasons to foster a sense of unworthiness as there are humans upon the Earth plane. It has been bred into most human cultures of your time to consider oneself unworthy unless one has sought redemption for one's "sins" in one manner or another. We do not say that this is a bad thing. Again, we cannot judge. But we have certainly noticed that this is a way one measures oneself in relation to other humans and ultimately to the Light: To decide whether one is "good" or "bad," i.e., worthy or unworthy of the Light.

When one chooses to believe that one is not worthy of the Light, one cannot find consolation within one's own soul. Consequently, one will turn to any other source of consolation in order to cope with the vicissitudes of life on Earth. In a world that can be replete with many sorrows, one may choose, for instance, an **addiction** to things such as money, mind-altering substances, sex, food, or superstitious beliefs that may seem to afford some comfort.

⅄ Koleje Loou

12

All of these addictions are then labeled "vices" by the many who may not understand the pain and fear that has led to such choices. We do not judge those who make these choices, nor do we judge those who judge those who make these choices. We cannot judge anyone, for we understand that **judgment may also be considered an addiction** that has its genesis in fear and pain.

From our perspective we do feel profound compassion for the loss of awareness that all humans can experience when they plunge into existence upon the Earth plane, forget that they are Light, and then choose to experience addiction in its many guises. We say "loss of awareness," because almost all human life on Earth at this time is an exercise in forgetfulness and then remembering.

So, you may be one who has forgotten that **the Light**, in which you may not believe, or of which you may not feel worthy, **is already within you**. It always has been, and always will be. Indeed, you can make the transition to another plane of existence, a process you call "death," and still not know that you carry this Light! But even after you experience what you call death, you will have the opportunity to remember that you are Light. At every moment the opportunities exist to awaken and know this truth about yourself.

Now, how are you afforded this opportunity to remember your truth, that you are this Light already, and therefore worthy of what you already possess? Well, there are many, many ways indeed, and more are being co-created by humanity and the Light in each moment. You see, as long as there have been humans upon the Earth plane, and as long as there has been forgetfulness, t opportunities to remember.

Now, most humans have not always relished and cherished these opportunities to remember. For as forgetfulness has become the predominant form of being upon the Earth plane, humans have made life for themselves increasingly difficult, devising weapons of mass destruction, harming each other indiscriminately and endeavoring to destroy the Earth that nurtures and sustains them. All of these behaviors have been driven by addictions such as those listed above. All have their genesis in fear, pain and suffering. For when one forgets the Light fear, pain and suffering will surely follow.

Most humans will believe that God (in His many forms upon the Earth plane) has ordained this suffering as punishment for man's sins. Not so; the Light is only benevolent and loving. **When humans forget the Light, they create their own suffering.** Awakening to the Light is the only way one can transcend suffering. And so, as humans have continually created ways to suffer, they have simultaneously created ways to awaken.

Until very recently in human time, suffering has been the most consistent catalyst to aid humans in choosing to remember and awaken. Now, it is becoming increasingly easier for humans to choose to remember without the degree of suffering that was once thought inevitable in the awakening process. You see, as the Earth plane is increasing in vibrational frequency, as discussed previously, it is far easier now than it has been in centuries of your Earth time to penetrate the veils between the higher frequencies and the Earth plane. Humans are beginning to have phenomenal experiences more easily. Therefore, they are more spontaneously finding the desire to awaken. You are living in very special times.

One of the ways in which humans have been experiencing these phenomena more easily is in connecting with the beings of Light who reside on higher vibrational frequencies. As we have stated, these beings are only here to be of service to you, to aid you in your awakening process. You have co-created them as you have co-created everything upon the Earth plane. Amazingly, their function in regard to you is the same as that of suffering: To help you know that you are Light. **By utilizing their help you can shorten the path of suffering**. This is truth.

As we have stated previously, there are many different categories of beings of Light that humans have co-created with the Light. That is the subject of this text.

Chapter 3

How do I Begin to Contact the Beings of Light?

Ask them for help. It is a simple truth. It is the human mind that chooses to complicate matters. The questions that come to your human mind upon hearing such a simple truth will be numerous. And, depending upon your history from this and other lifetimes (for indeed, you have lived other life times), you may choose to throw as many roadblocks in the way as you can create, consciously or unconsciously. You will ask: *Whom do I ask? How do I ask? When do I ask?* We will answer these questions in due time. The question, however, that will prove the most compelling is: *How will I know that they have heard me and that they will respond?*

The last question also may be the one that causes the most difficulty. Even if we tell you everything that you will ever need to know in order to access these benevolent beings -- and we shall endeavor to do this -- you will still wonder from time to time just how you can know that you have actually accessed this beautiful Light. You will ask more questions: *Is this my imagination? Can I trust this experience? Will there be some sign that is undeniable proof? Will others understand if I try to share this experience, or will they just think me mad?*

You will not be the first human who has ever asked such questions. Many brave souls before you have seen visions, heard voices, and tried to validate what has happened to them by sharing the experience with others.

Some have then been labeled mad, others have been persecuted, and still others have simply been called fools.

None of this is what you truly desire, yet something has compelled you to look at this book. Why? Could it be that somewhere inside you, you *do* know the truth? That truth is inviolable. Even if others might call you mad, you must find the answers for yourself. And we congratulate you for wanting to know.

Again, we say you are living in wondrous times, when it is easier than it has been in eons to access the other frequencies upon which these Light beings reside. It is also easier than ever to share with other humans what you are experiencing, without the calumny that might have once accompanied such disclosures. Indeed, your media have been full of such information in recent years. Have you wondered why the interest has accelerated? It is because those who have chosen to have such experiences have also chosen to share such with others.

Now, we must tell you that another being's experience will not be what happens to you when you begin to open to the beings of Light. It may be similar, but it will never be identical. **No two beings can have the same experience**. No two beings are completely alike, so it is impossible to have identical experiences. You are a unique individual, the composite of all you have experienced in this and other lifetimes. Relish your uniqueness and endeavor only to be open to what is possible for you.

Nor will we encourage you to tell others when you do have an experience. We cannot counsel you to do or not do anything, for this is a plane of free will, and as such you must

17

choose and decide for yourself.[1] We will, however, urge you to wait until you have finished reading this publication before you begin to open to your own personal experience. There are steps to be taken that can be most crucial to this experience for you. We may urge, request and counsel, but we can never direct you. You must direct yourself in your own unique fashion.

Indeed, we will counsel you on how to open to a connection with the beings of Light, and then we will counsel you to **expect nothing**. Whatever you might expect would only limit the possibilities of what you could experience. This is a most important point to keep in mind.

Also, do not try to repeat an experience that you may have had, for that, too, will limit what you could experience. If you are looking in one direction for one thing, while the connection will be happening another way, you might not even know that it has occurred!

What we are saying is that it is most important to **keep an open mind**. If you follow exactly what we describe here, **something will happen**. If your human mind, however, is filling with any of the aforementioned questions, or you are choosing to expect that something must happen in a certain way in order for it to be valid, then we can assure you that even though something will happen, you may never know that it did!

Thus we come to the **issue of trust**. This issue will be brought to your attention repeatedly, for it is most crucial. When the beings of Light come at your request, they do not

---

[1] Indeed, if a being from another vibrational frequency begins to insist that you do anything, we will urge you not to listen, for it will most likely not be a being with which you will experience your Highest Good. We will discuss this in more detail at another time.

come to prove themselves to you or to respond in an expected fashion. Beings of Light cannot prove themselves to you. For most of them, this is an incomprehensible concept. Since most have never been human, they do not understand how humans can doubt their existence. They know they exist and are here to be of service to you, and that is the only basis upon which they will respond. For you the leap of faith will be to trust that this is so. It is not for them to prove this to you in some test that will then create the faith in you. They can only connect with those who are willing to go into the experience without preconditions.

If you make a conditional request, stating that you will call on the beings of Light to help you once you know they are really there, then nothing, indeed, will happen, for you have made a precondition that they cannot fulfill. **If you do not trust with an open mind and ultimately with an open heart, then you will most definitely be disappointed.**

As we have stated before, humans continually give themselves opportunities for opening to the presence of beings of Light in response to an experience of suffering. Then and only then are most humans finally willing to try *anything* that might work, when everything upon the human plane has failed them.

We tell you, you do not have to wait until such a condition has befallen you. We offer you another way, if you will choose it.

19

Chapter 4

Sit and Be Still

In the "hustle-bustle" of this planet, it is most difficult for most humans to find time to stop, sit and be still. But that is exactly what is required to open easily to an awareness of the other frequencies of Light that are available. To tell you differently would mean not to speak the truth.

Yet, what we ask you to do, in order to know the beings of Light around you, may prove very difficult, indeed. Most humans are simply not prepared to sit quietly. Not to place a book before your nose, nor to turn to the plentiful forms of entertainment so easily available, will be your first challenge.

As we have said, only when these distractions, or the addictions we mentioned previously, no longer ease the suffering, will one usually concede that something else must be tried.

If you are one, however, who has blessed yourself with a burning desire simply to know, then sitting and being still will be a step that may come more easily to you. In any event, we will tell you that you can **ask for help** in developing the discipline of sitting! Indeed, this is a discipline, and help is available at every step of the way!

We do recommend, however, that you choose your place and time of sitting carefully. We have mentioned these things in our two previous publications with Leia,[1] but a simple reminder may be useful here.

- Find a place that is quiet and where distractions cannot arise easily.
- Choose a time of day when you may be more alert. For some, this will be upon arising. For others, it can be at any time of the day. But if one is tired, or already full of the day's events, simply sitting will prove more difficult.
- Choose a comfortable position. Many have learned postures from the meditative disciplines that support such experiences. We urge you, however, to adapt to what is comfortable for you. Our only request is that the spine be straight, the shoulders relaxed, and you be comfortable. Some find closing the eyes to be best. Others wish their eyes to be partially or completely open.
- Feel free to experiment until you find what is most comfortable to you. Other people may tell you that one must follow one certain way in order to be correct. We urge you to remember that you are a unique being of Light, and therefore able to ascertain for yourself exactly what will be most comfortable for you.
- Some will use incense, light a candle, or say a special prayer or chant in order to begin. Some may choose to sit before an altar where they have placed special, sacred items. Some may choose to hold a crystal. All those steps are fine for such an endeavor.

---

[1] See *Balancing the Light Within* and *Affirmations and Thought Forms*.

- Remember that intent is everything. This will be a form of meditation for *you*. If you hold that such an experience will be of the Light, then no matter how you create the experience, it will be of the Light.

And so you have sat, and you ask *What next?* It is possible that you are waiting for a miracle, or for something magical to happen. Indeed, your mind will most probably be filled with thoughts, for instance, the list of questions we have previously discussed. So, the next thing that we will ask you to do is to **empty your mind**.

Now, this may sound easy, but we will tell you that it is not. For most humans, once you realize that thoughts are racing through your mind, the thought of trying to stop them then becomes a thought, even an obsession. Thinking about how you will stop your mind from having thoughts simply compounds the matter.

Remember that you can **ask for help**. For the help to come to you, we strongly recommend that you create with your inner mind a force field, a vibrational frequency that will invite these beings of Light to come to you. We recommend that you simply begin to think about a beautiful Light. See its radiance surrounding and filling you with its healing and loving energy. This Light may be blue, violet, yellow, rose, magenta, green or white. Infuse the color that comes to you with a golden radiance. Relax into it as you gently breathe in and out. Expand the diaphragm with each breath in, and contract the diaphragm with each breath out. Let your breathing develop a comfortable rhythm.

Your thoughts will still come to you, and we ask you not to resist, but to allow such. Resistance will only create a struggle. As each thought comes, simply release it, and then remember to breathe in the Light that is coming to your inner mind.

And so you are simply relaxing and sitting in the Light. Allow it to fill your form and flow about you as you breathe it. Do not be concerned as to the origin of this Light. As we have said before, it has always been within you. In this moment of being still, you have chosen to acknowledge this Light within you, and you are consciously breathing it.

Also, do not be concerned regarding the color that has come to your awareness. As we have said before, this will be a unique experience for you, and so the color of which you become aware will be unique to you. Nor need you be concerned it the color that has come to your awareness changes to another. This is not uncommon. It simply means that one color is right for one moment, and another for another moment.

Some will see the color clearly. Others will not. This does not matter. If you have had a thought of it, it does exist whether you can see it clearly or not. This is simply how you co-create. You think a thought; an awareness comes to you, and then it exists.[1]

As you open to sitting in your Light, you may become aware that other colors are also part of what you are experiencing. These colors may be red, brown, orange, gray, or the absence of all color, black. These are not colors with negative value in and of themselves, for all is part of creation, and all creation originates in the Light. And we do not ask you to get rid of them, for you cannot. Nothing that exists or ever has existed can be destroyed, it can only change form.

---

[1] Our previous publication, *Affirmations and Thought Forms*, explains this concept in greater depth.

23

What we will suggest that you do at this time, however, is to change the appearance of such colors as you behold them. This can be done simply by asking for a violet Light to form a vortex. Then, in that vortex, allow the violet Light to mix with the other color or colors until these colors have become violet, also.[1]

As you work with the Angels and beings of Light, you may choose to do more with what you find when you go into "inner space." But for now, simply choose to create an opportunity to connect with the beings of Light consciously, allowing the brown, red, orange, gray and black to transform into a violet Light. If it is difficult, here, also, you may **ask for help** from the beings of Light. Simply ask, that is all you need do. If you do not see these colors (i.e., red, brown, orange, gray, or black), do not be concerned. But if you do, it may be useful to do what is described here.

So, you have chosen to sit and be still. You have created an awareness of a healing, loving radiance to surround and fill you, and have allowed yourself to concentrate upon this Light as the thoughts come and go within you. You are simply breathing and sitting. Now, it may be interesting to go into greater depth at this time to consider what has compelled you to endeavor to connect with the beings of Light in the first place! The answer to this and all other questions will be found in your heart.

Indeed, your mind may have many, many reasons why you have decided to know these beings of Light for yourself. These reasons may include what you have learned from the media, what other friends are doing, a desire to feel special because you can do this thing, or mere curiosity.

---

[1] Another previous publication, *Balancing the Light Within*, may provide more useful information in this regard.

Suffering and pain may have brought you to this point. Or, on a deeper level, there simply may be a compelling desire to know. Again, we do not judge any of these motives, for they are neither right nor wrong. They are simply the ostensible reasons that brought you to this sitting.

Now, we will ask you something you will think very strange. We ask you not to take any of these reasons seriously. If you do, you will create expectations leading to many more thoughts, thereby limiting what will be possible for you to experience. But more importantly, **the reasons of which your conscious mind is aware that bring you to this sitting, will never be the ultimate reason for why you do this thing. Your heart, and only your heart, knows the real reason.**

As you open to the beings of Light and begin to ask for their help, they will help you access what is deeply hidden in your heart, and the truth will be revealed to you. Be patient, dear ones, you will know the reason you are doing this thing when it is time. For now, we ask you to drop the reasons your mind has given you. Let them go, and just continue to bathe in and rest in the beautiful Light. Breathe, just breathe. You are learning to be in the moment, and that is essential to what you are endeavoring to do.

As we shared with you previously, beings of Light only know the moment. They do not reside within the limitations of time and space as you have chosen to do on the Earth. Therefore, they will work with you from moment to moment. Neither past nor future is truly relevant to them, although they can easily see and access information in both.

However, who you are, and how focused you are in the moment, is of utmost importance to them. If you are more focused on any of the thoughts or questions we have previously discussed, they cannot catch your attention as you attempt to open to them. It will be either difficult or impossible for them to do so. So, please, beloved friends, let the thoughts come and go. Just breathe in and out in the Light, and sit for now, in this moment, and then, in the next moment. Now you are ready.

Chapter 5

Who Will Come to Me?

The list is literally endless for each and every one of you! You are surrounded by many, many beings of Light. Some of you have had an experience already that has told you something is there that is not of this Earth plane. Others may simply wish to know if this really is true. But all who are reading this publication do so because *something* has compelled you to this moment of wanting to know more. That "something" is the Light, and the beings of Light which are already with you, and have always been with you. So, it is not a question of whether they are there for you. They are. They have brought you to this moment. Now it is time to find out a bit more about who they are for you.

Every human being is connected to beings of Light from every stratum of vibrational frequency currently available to Earth plane connection. There are vibrational frequencies with which humans cannot connect at this time. These frequencies are simply too high for human compatibility. The human body could not sustain such a connection. If you made the attempt and were at all successful, you would most likely disembody.

As it is, when you sit and breathe the Light, you are, in essence, altering the vibrational frequency of your body so that it may achieve access to what is available to you. That is why the exercise of sitting and breathing the Light is so essential to the process. Obviously, the more you are able to sit and be still while breathing the Light, the easier it will become to have an experience of the beings of Light. The old adage "practice makes perfect" definitely applies here. The more you try, the easier it will become. For some who have had years of practice, simply sitting for a moment or two is enough for a connection to be made. However, all who sincerely endeavor will succeed. You do not have to be special to do this thing. Sincerity and discipline are all that is required.

And so, let us tell you what already surrounds you. Picture, if you will, a most luminous **Light** that seems to be filled with every color of the spectrum. But it is not the same as the light that appears to your physical eyes. No, this Light possesses a quality unlike anything you will ever see while your eyes are open and you are in normal consciousness. The luminescent quality of this Light cannot be described in human terms. It is simply to be experienced as you sit. And yes, it will be different for each one of you as your own unique essence blends with the perfection of this Light. Do not be concerned if your inner vision does not see such a thing. We ask you simply to know that it is there. Eventually some kind of awareness will come. Be patient. It will come to you.

There will also be a **sound**, an indescribable sound that permeates all creation. It is the hum of creation. Each vibrational frequency has a different sound. As you change frequencies while sitting, you may, eventually, begin to notice the different sound that goes with each frequency. Some have called this sound the hum of the *Aum* or *Om*. Others perceive it as different pitches of ringing in the ears, as if bells were continuously being rung. Again, be open to how this will be for you. For now, we simply ask you to know that it exists and that it is possible for you to experience this sound with your inner hearing.

In addition to the background of this sound and Light, you have the possibility of connecting with the beings of Light who reside upon these different frequencies. As we have stated, you are connected with beings on all available strata. Your personal experience will depend on many factors. Uppermost will be your **karmic agreements** for this embodiment.[1] For the sake of brevity here, we will simply say that karmic agreements are the basis for the connections you have chosen to make in this embodiment. You agreed upon these connections with these specific beings of Light **before you were born**.

This is, indeed, worth noting, dear ones. Most probably you will have assumed that only if you are truly worthy, will such an experience as communicating with an Angel be possible for you. It is simply not as "glamorous" as you might suppose it to be. There is no judgment of one being more worthy than another. All are worthy. When you choose to remember your agreements with the beings of Light, you will know this to be true. What you choose to experience will simply be the actualization of an agreement of karmic origin. Since you are reading this, you may now be ready to fulfill that agreement.

While you have been moving through your life to this point, these beings of Light have never left your side. They have not left your side because, as we shared with you previously, beings of Light are not subject to the constraints of time and space as you are upon the Earth plane. They have no difficulty waiting. Indeed, they do not wait. This concept of "waiting" does not activate where they reside. Not only

---

[1] We have discussed the subject of karma in other publications throughout the centuries. We suggest that you investigate any of these publications if you have questions regarding such.

that, but while they have been with you, they have equally been able to be with everyone who has a connection with them.

They are not like pieces of pie, to be divided. Such a concept does not exist for them. They can be everywhere, always, with everyone because there is no time and space for them as you understand the concept. Interesting, is it not? We encourage you not to think about this too deeply, for the human mind will have difficulty comprehending such a thing. It is only important for you to comprehend that such is true.

Each being of Light, as it will connect with you, will have its own unique vibrational frequency, just as you do. As you become aware of the being with whom you have connected, you will form what may be called an electro-magnetic bond. Although it is not exactly the same thing, this is the easiest way to describe what happens. The connection will be similar in nature to an electro-magnetic bond as you have understood such upon the Earth Plane. The connection is made within your heart chakra.[1] There are hundreds of chakras ("wheels of Light") which connect the human body to a higher vibrational frequency that actually gives your body the Light which is its life-force. Many call this higher frequency your "Higher Self."

It is important to note here that the heart chakra is the central point for entry of all vibrational frequencies into your human body and awareness. Each chakra will carry much Light through it at various times, but it is always the heart that will be crucial and central to the very existence of the human form in time and space. So, as you sit quietly in a

---

[1] Chakras are described in greater depth in the publication *Balancing the Light Within.*

meditative state, we urge you to **open your heart and focus on what you sense here**.

Each being of Light, indeed, each being anywhere in creation, has what may be called its own electro-magnetic frequency. After a time you will begin to note a change in how your heart feels when you allow this Light to connect with you. You may call this special frequency for each being its "signature." If you cannot tell in any other way that you have made this connection, you can know how your heart feels differently as you are denoting the signature of the being of Light whom you have called to you.

One way to practice experiencing this is to think of a significant person with whom you have a relationship on the Earth plane at this time. It may be a sibling, spouse, parent or child. As you think of this person, you call his or her electro-magnetic force field to you. Yes, as we have said, all beings possess this force field, whether in human or other vibrational frequency.

You, too, have such a force field. It is the field of Light around and throughout your body. That is why, when you think of another, he or she very often is aware of this because the signature vibration of your force field has connected you to that person. To illustrate, think of the many times your telephone rings and you find yourself discussing how each was thinking of the other at that moment. You may laugh and say this is funny. But metaphysically it is in perfect order. When you think of another, you draw that electro-magnetic force field to you, and into your heart.

Now, at this very moment, as you think of this significant person in your life, how does your heart feel? It feels different from the way it feels at another time. You are feeling the electro-magnetic vibrational frequency of the person of whom you have just thought. That is that person's

31

"signature." And each time you think of this person, you will feel such a sensation.

It is very healing to infuse this connection with the thought of love for the other person, sent from your heart. The other will sense this. If you choose to send this love, however, do it without any expectation. Love is most powerful when offered unconditionally. When you expect something in return, the expectation negates the whole process immediately.

The same will be true when you open to the beings of Light who are connecting with your heart. Again, expect nothing. Allow your experience to be one of unconditional love from you to the being of Light, and from the being of Light to you. Don't limit the possibilities. Stay open. Simply note that the feeling in your heart will change. That is the signature of the being of Light connecting with you.

On the following pages we will discuss some of the possibilities of who may come to you. As we have stated before, there is no limit to what is possible. Remain open to what can be experienced.

Chapter 6

Archangels and Angels

You probably have heard and read many things regarding Archangels and their counterparts, the Angels. The legends and stories are numerous. Some stories are ancient. We are not here to tell you that there is one particular legend or story that associates these beings of Light with a particular God that is correct for everyone. Nor are we here to confirm that a certain hierarchy must be acknowledged when you seek to connect with them. That is not for us to do.

We do encourage you to investigate your personal belief system, and to acknowledge what resonates in your own heart, when you think of the Archangels and Angels. If a belief is important to you, then it is to be honored and acknowledged. There are no accidents in creation. If you have led yourself to know of the Archangels and Angels in a certain way, then this is important information for you to investigate. You may utilize that information to help you experience them personally, if you so choose.

You may assume that what you are drawn to know about the Archangels and Angels in this lifetime is information you also possessed in another incarnation. That is why that particular information will resonate with you now. As we have stated before, connecting with these beings of Light is an agreement you made before entering this embodiment. All you have learned and done to this point has occurred to prepare you to be aware of the existence of the Archangels and Angels, and then to desire a connection with them. If this means that a certain religious doctrine satisfies your understanding of these beings of Light, then for you this is valid and true to your experience at this time, and these beliefs are to be honored.

This also means that everyone else's belief systems are true as well. They are to be honored as yours is to be honored. **No one set of beliefs is true for everyone.** Humanity is diverse; that is how it has been created. To raise one set of beliefs above another harms everyone and can only continue to lead to the decimation of humanity. Hold strong to your beliefs if they are important to you. Honor your beliefs. And then honor everyone else's beliefs as important for them! Principally, all belief systems are capable of leading to the same Light. At their core, all great religions known to humanity at this time talk of the Oneness of All and everything, and affirm that All comes from one Creator-Source. These beliefs are crucial to one's comprehension of the Light. And that is important information to remember.

As we have stated previously, the Archangels and Angels came into existence because humanity needed a way to connect with the Light from human form. As humanity moved away from knowing the true nature of All and everything, it became more and more difficult for the human mind to conceptualize one's essence as Light and what this could mean to those walking the Earth plane. Consequently, human beings yearned to remember, to know why they had become human and to understand the mysteries of life and death. As an answer to the earliest forms of prayer expressing such yearnings, the beings of Light came into existence.

In those early times, it was easy to see that miraculous things could occur, such as the birth of a child. But it was also easy to see that the Earth could become a hostile environment very quickly, bringing about suffering and death. So, religions and philosophies developed to try to explain why such things occurred. Humanity was trying to make sense of things, and trying, through prayer, to control the course of events.[1] Thus, the beings of Light were co-created from a blending of the Light of the Creator-Source with the prayer and longing of humanity. Humanity's prayers were answered.

ARCHANGELS

And so, the Archangels were created and became what they are today, another aspect of reality for many, many humans. In the continuous process of co-creation humanity infused them with even more power, which is why Archangels have the most powerful force-field available to humans at this time. Because of the power of this Light, a word of advice is in order: We will tell you that it is most crucial when invoking these beings, to do so with the purest intent and motive and the most wisdom that you can summon. This is crucial to interaction with *all* of the beings of Light. For if one were to summon their help for nefarious reasons, one would find that, indeed, one's prayers would be answered. But perhaps not as one had hoped!

The beings of Light will come to you to aid only in what can be called the Highest Good for all and everything. So, if your request is not for the Highest Good, it will be noted -- and, for your own Highest Good, you may experience what you intended for another. It may be well to remember that **whatever you send forth into creation will return to you manifold.** We do not ask you to have

---

[1] While the better part of wisdom would be to trust, which would eliminate the need to control, this is much easier said than done for most humans at this time.

expectations of how this will occur. Again, it is important to remember that expectations are limiting. But we will tell you that if you request for another, you will also receive that which you have requested.

Archangels have never been in human form, and therefore they have never been subject to the vagaries of human existence. They are neither male nor female, but are beings who embody the purest form of Loving Light available to humans at this time, beyond the dichotomy of the sexes. Some of the religions of the world conceptualize that the Archangels were the original co-creators of all that is perceived as creation. As such they are the most direct link to the Light that is available to humanity in its purest and most powerful form.

And so, you have been drawn to the Archangels. Perhaps this has been a lifelong affinity. On some level you may feel that you already know them well. Their power has been described to you as formidable. You may have been taught in the Western tradition that Lucifer[1] was the one who fell from God's grace and single-handedly created all that is considered evil when he turned his back to the Light; therefore, he is no longer of the Light, and unsuitable to be summoned to aid you. Or that Michael was the one who strode forth to defend all of humanity from this evil. Or that it was Gabriel who informed Elisabeth that she would give birth to John the Baptist, and Mary that she would carry Jesus, the son of God. And so forth and so on.

You may wonder how you, a simple mortal, can dare to feel such profound affinity and sense of connection to these beings of Light, whose legendary power is beyond comprehension. Are you in a position to claim your

---

[1] Latin: the Light-bringer

36

connection? And, if so, who is it that you would call? Would your reasons be sufficient to summon them to you? Would they find your request acceptable and actually respond? Perhaps you already have had an experience of these magnificent beings of Light, and now you have difficulty believing that such could have actually happened to you.

These are questions that are common when humans endeavor to contact beings whom they have been trained to worship and hold in awe. But we will tell you that these beings of Light do not require worship. Indeed, they find such activity often interferes with their usefulness to you. You still may feel that there must be some sort of protocol you need to follow before they will find a connection with you acceptable. We say again, if your belief system specifies that some sort of activity is necessary before you summon these beings, then it may be wise for you to follow your belief system if it resonates with you. However, if you do not so choose, you will not be damned or ignored. You will still be loved by all the beings of Light as you have always been loved, and they will respond to your call no matter how trivial the setting may seem to you.

The truth, beloved ones, is that the Archangels are here to serve you, not to cause you fear that, if you do something incorrectly, it will provoke their disapproval. They were co-created to serve you and all humanity. They have *always* been with you. This will never change, no matter how your human mind tries to imagine the situation.

The Archangels are here to serve you, and to aid you in opening to a greater awareness of who you are. They are here to help you awaken to the true nature of your being and the true nature of All and everything. They have always been with you, one lifetime after another, for this very reason. They are loving, kind, compassionate and generous. They do not judge you. Indeed, this is a human concept they cannot comprehend or act upon.

So, how does one request a connection with an Archangel? We will suggest an exercise that may be useful. We do not tell you that this is something you must do in order to be correct. Absolutely not. We do say that these suggestions can be useful if you choose to follow them. But they are *not* crucial to your connection to the Archangels. Listen to your hearts and follow your own inspiration, beloved ones, to ultimately know what is right for you.

Sit, and be still. Then, if you wish, request that a pyramid of golden Light descend about your being, encompassing the four sides around you. Gently breathe in the healing radiance that such a configuration will create. Once you are comfortable, inside that which you have created with your inner awareness, request that the Archangels secure the pyramid surrounding you. Call them by name. If names do not come easily, then we suggest the names of Michael, Raphael, Gabriel and Uriel (or Ariel). Ask each one to take a side of the pyramid, securing it in your space and time.

As you call each Archangel, allow your heart to open, to feel the Light and love of this being enter your heart. Say each name slowly and easily. After speaking each name, sit and breathe through your heart as the loving Light of each Archangel pours into it. Take in this loving energy. Drink it in and simply continue to breathe as you allow each loving presence to fill you.

One or two Archangels may resonate for you more profoundly than others. That is fine. You may simply have a greater karmic connection with these. This is not uncommon. All are powerful beings of Light. What resonates for you personally, inside your own heart, is all that need matter to you. Once you have become aware of the connection that feels most profound to you, during subsequent encounters you may leave yourself open to allow these beings to come to you more directly.

In the beginning it may be useful to invoke the Pyramid of Light before requesting the connection with the Archangel(s) to whom you feel most connected. Eventually, you may be comfortable invoking their presence at any time by simply calling a name and requesting help. You may come to find this a very comforting and wondrous experience.

Now, once you have established a sense of this loving Light within your heart, what will you request? Do not be shy, dear ones. As we have said, the Archangels are here to be of service to you. They will always answer your request in the wisest way; they cannot do otherwise. Keep in mind, however, that whatever you request must be for the Highest Good, and in service to the Light. You may, for instance, request help in your awakening process. Or you may ask to be healed.[1] You may ask for help in the healing of others. You may ask for greater compassion, greater wisdom, or greater comprehension of that which you wish to know to further your awakening process. Or you may simply ask for help.

One way to know what it is that you wish to ask, is when you find yourself in a situation where your human mind cannot find an answer. This is a way the Light within

---

[1] In our previous publication, *Balancing the Light Within*, we explain that all human beings who are on the Earth plane at this time have a need for healing.

39

you allows you to know that it is time to ask for help. How many times have you sat with what you perceived to be a problem without a solution? In such instances, simply ask for help and wait. An answer will come. When you invoke the aid of these wondrous beings of Light, no task is too small. No matter is too insignificant. Remember, these beings are here to help you awaken. If the matter seems important to you, then it *is* important!

After you have asked for help, and felt the Archangels' loving energy in your heart, know that you can sit and be still, and perhaps even hear a response. This will not come as words, but as thoughts. These thoughts will not request that you act in a certain way. Indeed, if you hear a response to that effect, then it most probably will be your own human mind speaking back or the voice of a different type of vibrational being who wishes to work through you. We will address such a situation at another time. For now, simply know that you do not need to honor such a request.

The kind of response you may receive from the Archangels will include a request to **remember that you are loved**. To remember that the **Archangels are here to be of service** to you. To remember that **your request has been heard**. To remember to **trust that all is in perfect order**, and that **all will unfold in that perfect order**. When you find yourself in the middle of a difficult situation, you may not realize that this could be so. From the middle, there is no perspective. However, these beings of Light possess that perspective. As you open to listening, they will offer that perspective to you. Be patient, continue to practice what is comfortable for you as you sit in meditation, and know that you are surrounded by beneficent beings who are here to help you in every moment you request their help.

Again, make your requests without expectation of how the response will come. Simply request and then let go. Let go and trust. The trust is crucial. Staying open to the response is crucial. Know that the whole experience of sitting, requesting and connecting will be healing to you if you allow it. Be still, be kind to yourself by opening yourself to this experience, and trust.

ANGELS

The Angels are also a great blessing to humanity. They, too, were co-created to be of service to you and to aid you in your awakening process. As with the Archangels, many legends and stories have come to you about these beings. In the West, a renewed interest has been fueled by stories of phenomenal experiences that individuals have shared with others.

What is it that you can believe for yourself regarding these wondrous beings of Light? Many of you have heard of certain hierarchies associated with them. According to various traditions, there are seraphim, cherubim, devas and so forth. Then there are the guardian Angels that you have heard are assigned to each and every one of you. We will speak of the guardian Angels in a separate chapter, for there is much to comprehend in this regard. Suffice it to say that they do not actually belong to what we will discuss here.

In regard to how one comprehends Angels in general, we will simply suggest, once again, that you reflect on what you already know about these beings. If you have been led to a certain set of beliefs, and they resonate with you, then these beliefs are what you wish to know in this lifetime in order to further a connection with the Angels. What you know is valid and true for you. It may not be true for everyone, just as another's truth may not be valid for you. As we have stated previously, all beliefs are to be honored. One can access these beings as one wishes based on what one knows. The Angels are simply here to love and to be of service to you. It matters not where you place them in the hierarchy. If a connection and/or an experience is profound for you, then honor what you know to be your reality. This honoring of your beliefs in and of itself will be healing and transformational for you.

Many experiences that have been attributed to the Angels may, indeed, have involved non-angelic beings of Light who have seemed like Angels to humans because the encounters were "otherworldly." Often, these are beings from other vibrational frequencies who were able to make their presence felt by human beings. The fact that these beings are not Angels does not invalidate such experiences. We will provide further explanation about those beings in a later chapter.

What are the attributes of Angels you would wish to comprehend? They have been characterized as being in service to God or, as we would say, to the Light. As with the Archangels, Angels have never been embodied, in human form or otherwise, and so have not been subject to the vagaries that embodiment would bestow. They are neither male nor female, because they have never had a physical form. They are here for your Highest Good, and will hear and answer all requests with the loving, healing presence of their Light.

As you continue to open and awaken to the Light, you will call them to you more easily and frequently. As you allow these connections to occur, the number of Angels in your company will continuously increase. Some have referred to this as an "expanding aura" surrounding you while you awaken and open. It can, indeed, be perceived as such. This is the main function that Angels perform for you. Afford yourself the opportunity to know that this is true.

You become a more powerful being of Light in human form as you welcome the Angels to you, and request their help in meditation and prayer. Know that they will respond. You do not need to call them by name. Names do not matter to them. It is human beings who have a need for names. The Angels recognize all parts of creation by their frequencies, and by the Light emitting from everything.

There is an angelic counterpart to all that one can perceive in creation. As you observe a rose blossoming, understand that an angelic counterpart, which some of you would call a deva, is filling this rose with love and Light as it blossoms. Your Angels do the same for you.

And so, as you blossom, allow yourself the gift of an awareness that your whole world is permeated by the angelic realm. Angels are not far away from you, not looking down upon you from some "heavenly" realm. Indeed not. What would be the usefulness of such a remote observation to humanity? These **beings of Light are permeating all of creation** with their blessings of love and Light. All you need do, to begin to know this, is call upon them.

In opening to these beautiful beings of Light, allow what you already know to be your guide. If you wish to utilize a pyramid of Light in which to make your initial contact, this would be quite useful. What has been previously written regarding such a pyramid of Light can also be applied in accessing the Angels. As you sit quietly, simply open your heart to feel this connection. Ultimately, you will come to know that you can ask any time and in any space, and you will feel the beauty of this connection come to you. Cherish and rejoice in the experience.

Unlike Archangels, Angels will not transfer specific thoughts to you in response, for they do not possess such a capability. Rather, they will fill you with their loving radiance, and you will be comforted and healed, if this is what you allow yourself to experience. Eventually, you may also become aware of these beings with your inner and/or outer senses as wondrous sound and luminous Light. Leave yourself open to such possibilities. Be still, be patient, be open to allowing your aura to expand with their loving, healing Light, and trust.

Chapter 7

Beings of Light - Ascended Masters

Now you are entering the realm of those beings who have had physical embodiments and who no longer need to experience being human as part of their awakening process. These beings previously achieved complete spiritual awakening while in human form. Now they choose to offer their Light to the rest of humanity from the higher vibrational frequencies upon which they currently reside.

From time to time some of these beings have resumed human form, enabling others to see by their example how one can awaken and ascend as they have done. Those beings who have chosen such a path have been called by many terms throughout history, such as *bodhisattvas*, *avatars*, *Buddhas*, or saints. Some Enlightened Ones have chosen to be examples for humanity and to play a role in the creation and sustaining of the major religions of the World.

We, who have agreed to collaborate with Leia in the publication of these manuals, are also of this realm. We have had many, many Earth embodiments, and have frequently chosen to return to the Earth in order to be of service to others who wish to awaken and who have requested our aid. At this particular time, however, we have chosen to remain in the higher vibrations, as it is easier now than it has been in eons for humans to achieve access to our frequencies. During this time of great and wondrous change upon the Earth plane, humans can benefit from connection to and interaction with our frequencies far more easily than before. You have chosen to live in magnificent times, dear ones, and publication of these manuals is one evidence of what is available to all of you, if you so choose it.

The important thing to remember is that **we are still with you today, all of us.** We are still available for you to call upon us at any time. We are beneficent beings of Light, here to be of service to you, as are the Archangels and Angels. You do not need to worship or adore us in order to call forth our love and Light. There is no need to appease us or to follow any particular prescribed ritual before engaging us. However, as we have spoken before, if it comforts you to engage in prescribed ritual, then, by all means, do so. We simply wish to emphasize that such is not necessary in order to request help from the many loving beings of Light.

Please be assured that we would never judge whatever ritual you may desire to employ in endeavoring to connect with us. However, we suggest that initially this connection may be accomplished most easily by sitting in quiet meditation and opening yourself to the higher frequencies. Remember to invoke a safe space such as asking for a pyramid of Golden Light and the presence of the Archangels. This may be most useful in creating a force field conducive to a connection. As we have stated, we are with you always, so it is only a matter of asking to be made aware of our presence as you sit quietly and invoke the Light.

Now, why would you wish to ask for us? Would not an Archangel or Angel be powerful enough to be of service to you? The answer is yes; any invocation of any being of Light is enough. It is simply a question of what you are drawn to know in this embodiment. That will decide for you whom you wish to call. If you have been drawn to know about the Ascended Master realm, or about a certain Ascended Master, then your desire will be to connect with such. Honor what you have learned as you have progressed through lifetime after lifetime, and honor what you feel drawn to know and do.

If you are drawn to a certain Master, then that is because you have known this being before in another embodiment. You and the Master may have been in physical form simultaneously, or the Master may have been in ascended form while you were in the physical. Either way, you have been together before, and now you wish to be together again.

In most instances, you agreed, before you came into this embodiment, to seek this connection again. You have been drawn to this time and space because you are ready to activate this agreement. Often you may have an affinity for more than one Ascended Master. If this is the case, then allow yourself to endeavor a connection with more than one.

Please be aware that it is you who will be doing the choosing. We are here for everyone who wishes to make a connection with us. If you were to think that you are more special than another because you have chosen to establish a connection, then this may lead to some confusion for you. **Everyone is special. No one is more special than any other.**

Knowing that everyone is special may work in your favor, if you are one who is given to believe that you are not special enough for such a connection. Understand that it is not a question of earning any special merit in order to experience such a connection. Leia wishes to insert here that when someone asks her why such a connection occurs for her, she usually answers that she needs it more than others. Of course this is not true. None is more special. And none need it more. We are here for everyone at any time. If you are drawn to us, and allow your heart to open to such an awareness, then we will automatically be drawn to you.

47

Simply open yourself to a connection, and sooner or later it will be known to you.

When you have made a connection with us, it is likely to bring a feeling of great comfort as you allow this loving Light to first fill your heart, and then your being. It may begin as a tingling sensation, a warmth, or a feeling of fullness. You are filling with a higher vibration of Light than you have ever consciously allowed yourself to know before. Relax into it. Allow the questions generated by your mind to dissolve as you simply open to the feeling. Emotions may arise, as well. Honor them as they come up. Allow yourself to feel whatever you may feel. Give yourself time to become used to the experience. There is no need to do anything. Just sit and be still. **Allow!**

In time, you may notice that thoughts come to you. Allow them. By this means, the Ascended Masters will attempt to communicate with you. The first thoughts they send will be of their love for you. They will wish to share with you that you are loved and ask if you are willing to open your heart as much as possible to this awareness. If you allow it, this will be healing to you. They may wish to let you know that they are with you at all times. They may remind you that all you need to do is ask for this awareness.

Do not be alarmed or afraid, for they cannot come to you unbidden. Yours is a plane of free will, so they can only come when asked. If they do come, and you are not aware of having made a request, be assured that on some level, whether consciously or not, you did make such a request. In that case, it most probably occurred before this lifetime.

Whether your request was conscious or not, once you have established an awareness, please allow yourself to know that this is a time for great awakening and opening within you. Another part of your being, your own totality or Higher

Self,[1] has helped to bring you to this moment. **Your Higher Self is another portion of the being of Light that is you**. This may be difficult for you to comprehend, so we will just ask that you trust that this is so. When we come in service to you, we are here to aid you in awakening to this very awareness of your own Higher Self. This will be a process. It is a process of learning everything about yourself that is pertinent to your awakening to your own Higher Self. It is a process of healing all that you hold in fear or pain within, so that the Light of your Higher Self may flow easily and unobstructed through your being. This is **Enlightenment**. We have gone through this process ourselves, and now we are here to be of service to you as you choose to experience the same process!

On your journey to this awakening, you will discover many things about yourself. You will learn that you are loved and cared for. You will learn that all requests for help from the Light are answered. You will learn to trust. You will gain wisdom and compassion for yourself and the All and everything. You will comprehend peace. You will understand all that is creation, and the Source of that creation. And you will trust your own Light to guide you in all that you choose to experience while being human.

Now you may say that this seems impossible to achieve while human. We say it is not. We have done it. We were no more gifted than you when we began our journeys to this awakening. And we cannot judge whether one is more worthy than another to proceed on this journey. However, we can respond to your requests, and we will aid you with total unconditional love as you begin an awareness that this is

---

[1] We will go into greater detail regarding your Higher Self at another point in this publication.

what you have chosen to do as well. The journey can be arduous, and so, much love has been co-created to help you along the way. We are part of that love and Light that is here to help.

In this simple publication we cannot list all the beings in the Ascended Master realm who have agreed to be of service to all of humanity at this time. Their number is legion. However, for the sake of orientation, and to help you grasp the nature of these beings, we will mention a few who are well known to many of you. They are listed in no special order of importance, for they would not desire to be ranked. They see their Light and all Light as one and the same, perfect and whole.

Some Ascended Masters are: Jesus the Christ; Gautama Buddha; Mary, mother of Jesus; Joseph, father of Jesus; Avilokitesvara; Kwan Yin; Mohammed; the Buddhas; the Saints of every faith; the beings ascribed to the Great White Brotherhood; Emissaries of Light; the great Avatars, Yogis, and Masters of every faith.

Again, if you have chosen to be aware of certain beings who have lived and then ascended, and you feel an affinity for those beings, then these are ones you have known before, and wish to connect with again. Open your heart, dear one; allow that love to pour into you, and accept our support as you awaken.

Continue to be aware, also, that your experience of the Ascended Masters will be unique to you. We have described in general terms what will be possible. But because you are a unique being of Light, your relationship with us will be unique. You have your own karmic history with the Ascended Masters, and that will definitely contribute to what you choose to experience with us in this embodiment.

Leia is willing to share that she works primarily with El Morya Khan, St. Germain, the Christ Light, and the Light of Ma (i.e., the Divine Mother energy), because she has the strongest karmic and emotional connections to these beings. Before entering this embodiment, she agreed to consciously connect with these Ascended Masters once she fulfilled other karmic agreements upon the Earth plane. Those experiences then left her open to a desire to know more about these beings.

In her particular instance, at the age of 39 she was awakened from her sleep to behold herself enfolded in a healing frequency of Light. She experienced a state of bliss that she had never before known upon the Earth plane. In fact, we had communicated with her in this manner many times previous, while she had been in dream state. But it was not until this moment that she was ready to become consciously aware of such. Without words, simply with thought, we communicated with her, to let her know that all was in perfect order, that she was doing quite well, and that she need not be concerned. We reminded her that she was loved beyond any love that she had ever consciously known.

It seemed to Leia that we had come unbidden. But this was not so. Every time she had prayed, or asked for help, we had answered her. Now she would consciously know this to be so. It had been agreed, before her incarnation that she would become consciously aware of us at a certain time in her life upon the Earth plane. She chose to keep that agreement. If you are drawn to the beings of Light, know that you have made a similar agreement.

We are communicating with you now. Once you open to allowing this awareness into your conscious mind, you will know this to be true.

Chapter 8

Disembodied Beings of Light and "Guardian Angels"

What do we mean by "disembodied beings of Light"? This does sound a bit strange, does it not? Some may choose to call these beings "ghosts" or "spirits" who have remained near the earth plane to stay with humans after the end of their corporeal lives. Some humans may believe these beings to be frightening when viewed in relation to the normal reality one perceives on a daily basis. We are here, dear ones, to help you comprehend the true meaning of who and what these beings are and who they can be in relation to you.

Let us begin with a basic understanding of "disembodied." This simply means "energy without a physical form upon the Earth plane." If these energies are higher vibrational in nature, they may be Angels, Archangels or Ascended Masters. In this context, however, we speak of human beings who have gone through the process that you call "dying," and who no longer inhabit human form. This does not mean that they are dead. Not in the least. They no longer have physical bodies, and therefore are not as easily perceivable with your senses as they once were when they inhabited the Earth plane. But they still have life force, which we call "I⋅ "

you to comprehend that there is no such thing
⋅u have been trained to understand it in your
Nothing dies, it just changes form, actually
'he condition it had before birth, with the
'ing on Earth has added to the form. The

form is now one of Light without body. Hence, the term "disembodied beings of Light" may be appropriate here.

Any of the beings of Light discussed in previous chapters, such as Angels, Archangels, and Ascended Masters, may very easily be designated as true Guardian Angels. However, most who feel they have had an encounter with a "Guardian Angel" are likely to have experienced one of these disembodied beings of Light. The term "Guardian Angel" is somewhat of a misnomer as these beings do not truly belong to the angelic realm. However, the term has been widely used among humans and so we feel a need to explain the significance of this phenomenon.

Most of the reported experiences attributed to Angels are actually stories regarding "Guardian Angels," nonphysical beings stepping in to offer protection, help, healing, love or advice when one most needed it. They are disembodied beings of Light who are with you to guide and protect you from the vicissitudes of life. You may never be consciously aware of a "Guardian Angel's" existence, but somehow you may sense his or her presence when you need it most. These beings' vibrational frequencies are still relatively close to your frequency, and so it is easier for them to touch you in a profound way that you can sense fairly easily.

Who could these beings be in relation to you? Most often, they are beings who have known you in your current lifetime. You probably had a close, personal connection, and now that this being has disembodied, he or she still chooses to be connected to you.

Most frequently the connection on the Earth plane was one of profound love, leaving one or both parties with a feeling that there is unfinished business between the two of you. The one left behind on the Earth plane often continues to grieve well after the "death" of the departed one. Each time you think of the one who has departed you call this being back to you.

As with all the beings of Light, all you need do is think of a disembodied being of Light, and he or she is drawn to you, whether you wish to consciously acknowledge such or not. These beings will feel free to openly and easily respond to this connection with you, provided they are also feeling drawn to you.

Disembodied beings of Light and "Guardian Angels" do.come unbidden; you need not request their intervention in your life. Most of these beings have been in human form fairly recently, in relation to Earth time; they have not yet chosen enough higher vibrational awareness to cease their need and desire to be of direct service and connection to those who are still embodied. They are not obliged to follow the protocol of higher vibrational beings of Light.[1]

Because the vibrational frequency of the Earth plane is increasing continuously -- narrowing the gap to the nonphysical planes -- contacts between humans and disembodied beings of Light will become ever more easily accomplished. Such connections happen more frequently than any of you realize. Since this interference is essentially continuous, it is most important that you comprehend thoroughly how best to utilize such connections for your growth in awakening to the Light within.

Let us give you an example. Your Grandmother was delighted at your birth, instantly loved you because of a profound karmic connection, and wished to be with you as you grew, so that she could contribute her knowledge and

---

[1] One of the hallmarks of higher vibrational beings of Light is their absolute respect of the law of Free Will.

love to you. But because of her karmic agreements, she chose to die when you were still in infancy. She transitioned before she could fulfill her heart's desires in regard to you -- and before you ever had a conscious awareness of her as a person. Consequently, she has stayed close to the Earth plane, even though she no longer has a body.

When she was in a body she had been able to comprehend enough about the Light to subsequently reach a certain level of awareness on the higher planes. She desires to share with you the Light she now carries, and she offers herself to you in support of your awakening process. She will whisper to you in your sleep, tell you to stop when you do not see the traffic light, tell you whom you should marry, remind you to call your parents and generally encourage you to be a good, healthy, happy soul while you are alive. She may also choose to worry about you when she feels you have done something wrong or are not well. Whether you have the ability to be aware of her presence or not, on some level, you will feel her influence as well as the influence of all the disembodied beings who seek to maintain connection with you. This unseen influence has contributed to every aspect of your life and to who you are now.

Let us give you another example. You and your spouse divorced under rather strained circumstances. There is no love between you, at least not to your conscious awareness. In fact, you could say at times that you have hated this person. Your former spouse chooses to disembody before you have come to terms with your strong feelings. However, due either to your continuing thoughts of this person, or your former partner's continuing feelings for you, you find that a profound emotional connection still exists, and it is making you unhappy. This connection is affecting your life, even though the person is "dead." Remember, there is no death as understood in the western tradition. Emotions continue to be felt by a disembodied being even after the body has become inanimate.

Now, we are sure that you would prefer the connection with Grandmother to the connection with the former spouse. But what about the times when Grandmother is worrying about you, and sending messages of advice that you may not feel would be most helpful to you? We will help you understand what you can do about this.

If you have chosen to develop some psychic abilities in your lifetime, you may think that any information that you receive from another plane should be followed because it is from "up there," and therefore automatically of greater value than what you receive "down here." We are here to tell that this is simply **not true**. And we do hope you heed this counsel. Not all that you receive from other vibrational frequencies will be useful to you. In fact, the contrary may be true. **We urge you to be very discriminating in what you choose to receive.** Verify the source of the guidance and decide whether it is right for you, before you choose to accept and act upon what you hear. Later on in this publication we will explain in greater detail how this can be done. Because you have lived literally thousands of times before, the karmic connections you have within the Earth plane, and with other vibrational frequencies, are countless.[1] You would be wise to develop a capacity to discriminate for yourself when you choose to access other planes of reality and become aware of what can be available to you. Undoubtedly, there is an abundance of support available

---

[1] We will not delve into the profound experiences and insights one can gain when one chooses to access other worlds of existence. This would be the subject for another publication.

from higher planes. But there are also many confused beings, such as the spouse or the Grandmother mentioned above, who will want to access your time and space because of a desire to advise you or affect you in some way.

What can you do in this regard? As we have stated, to be discriminating is the first order of business. How best can this be accomplished? We suggest that you consider a simple "litmus test" that will help you to determine what will be useful in your awakening process, and will help you to let go of what may not.

Suppose you have stilled your mind, invoked a safe healing radiance to enfold you, and have successfully connected to another vibrational frequency. From lack of experience, perhaps, you have left yourself open to encountering any being of Light, without stipulating that it be one from a higher frequency (such as an Angel, Archangel or Ascended Master). You may sense a presence; perhaps, the Light has become different, or you are perceiving a sound or feeling. You begin to have thoughts or hear words that do not seem your own. You are intrigued. How can you be sure that what you are sensing will aid you in awakening and healing? This is the "litmus test" that we would recommend:

- *Always* invoke a healing radiance to enfold you before you open your consciousness. If you then sense that the Light has changed to a duller, darker color, take note. If there is a great deal of red, brown, black or gray, or the color has become murky, then you have attracted a being that has not yet opened to an awareness of the Light in a way that would be useful to you.
- If the being begins to give you any kind of direct order to perform an action, pursue a line of thought, or undertake anything that might be harmful to yourself or another,

57

then you can be sure that you are not in contact with a being who wishes your highest and best. This is a plane of free will choice; you can be assured that beings on higher vibrational frequencies would not order you to do anything. Most certainly they would never suggest that you harm yourself or another.

- If either of these two conditions exists, then we counsel you to ask further: *Are you here for my Highest Good?* and *Are you of the Light?* According to cosmic law, any being must answer both questions. At times some lower vibrational beings may answer "yes" to the first and "no" to the second question, or they may not answer at all, or answer in an evasive manner. If the answer is anything but a straightforward "yes" to both questions, or, inside yourself, you sense that this being is either not here for your Highest Good, or not of the Light, then you can order it away from you and into the Light. And it must go. This is cosmic law.

Ordering a Being into the Light

First, remember that this is a plane of free choice, and nothing from other vibrational frequencies can be with you or affect you if you do not choose to permit it. You may encounter many kinds of disembodied beings when you begin to open. **Be aware that you have free choice to decide with whom you wish to be connected.** This can be most important and useful information for you to know. Many humans do connect with other beings without awareness that they have done so, and then wonder what is happening that is making their lives more difficult than necessary. To be forewarned is to be forearmed. It can be quite simple to send a being to the Light for further healing and awakening, and thus to free yourself of an influence with which you do not wish to contend.

Here are some simple steps to take:

First, do not be afraid, dear ones. What we tell you is useful and helpful, and can have a most healing affect upon you, enabling you to discover and strengthen your own power of choice. If a fear does come to you, however, honor it, and ask for healing for what you are feeling. Never deny or ignore what you are feeling. It will not go away. Simply acknowledge it, and request healing from the Light. Be open to allowing such a healing to occur.[1]

- Breathe in the Light as you open to contact with the being that you wish to move into the Light.
- As you begin to create a safe space of Light and love about you, you may use an incense or herb to help you. [2]
- Ask for higher vibrational beings of Light such as Angels, Archangels, and Ascended Masters to come to your awareness and help you with this healing process. Since these higher vibrational beings are always with you, it is simply a matter of asking for a conscious awareness of their presence.
- Visualize a pyramid of Light forming about you, and then request that a vortex of golden-white Light fill your space. Invite the being for which you desire further awakening and healing into the vortex. This vortex will create a powerful force field that will attract the being to it. Ask the higher vibrational beings of Light to escort said being into the vortex. If you wish, you may tell the

---

[1] There is much useful information in our previous publication, *Balancing the Light Within,* that can aid you in this process.

[2] Leia suggests that sandalwood and/or sage may be the incense and herb of choice.

being it may return to you in time. However, before it may return, the being must allow for a time of healing and cleansing. After you have invoked the vortex of golden-white Light, ask your heart when it is time to let the vortex, and the beings within it, depart from your time and space. And then let it go.

- Continue to request transformation and healing for all emotions and feelings that will come to you as you initiate this process. Since you may have known this being in this life, and many past lives as well, many thoughts, feelings and emotions may come to you. Of course, there are no accidents in Creation, and this being has come to you to further a healing process for both parties, if you wish it. So, as you send the being forth for its healing, you may also afford yourself the same![1]
- Be aware, each time you return to thoughts of this being, a portion of its energy will return to you, and so, continued requests for healing may be most useful for you and this being. When your thoughts become clear and peaceful regarding this being, you will know that the healing has become complete, and further communication will now be possible, if you so desire.

Now, we ask you to be aware that many beings may wish to come to you who will not have a detrimental effect upon you! They will simply wish to assist you in your awakening and healing process, out of unconditional love for you. They will have no other agenda, and they will desire nothing other than to aid you in co-creating your own Highest Good. These are beings who have become awakened

---

[1] Again, our previous publication, *Balancing the Light Within,* holds much useful information in this regard.

enough in their lifetimes, or while in higher vibration, to wish to be of service. They may not have the developed gifts of an Ascended Master, but what they have to offer can be quite profound. These are the beings who would most appropriately be called "Guardian Angels," if you wish to use the term.

They may wish to warn and advise you more directly than a Master would, however. In that event, we urge you again to exercise your free will in responding to their direct dialogue with you. After establishing a conscious communication with such a being, it may be wise to also establish rules of cooperation, pertaining when and where you will permit this communication. Some humans set certain times, or enact ritual that will allow the being to know when it is welcome in their space.

Some humans choose to write out the information they receive, in order to absorb it more easily and perhaps to share with others what they are learning. For instance, you may wish to share with others what you have learned in healing or "channeling"[1] sessions. Others have used the information they have received for the purpose of creating works of art, music, poetry and literature. Again others have been inspired to great inventions, or moved to perform valuable public service. Your cultures are replete with examples of such fruitful collaboration. **All things are possible, beloved ones, when you allow your heart to be**

---

[1] Channeling is a process which includes opening one's self to information perceived from higher vibrational sources and expressing this information, either through writing, speaking or artistic/creative expression. Furthermore, one can channel Light for healing purposes such as laying on of hands. The information or Light may stem from your own Higher Self or from other beings of Light.

open and accept the infinite love and Light available to you in a safe, healing space.

Chapter 9

Twin Flame and Soul Mates

Because of the profound interest that has been generated upon the Earth plane regarding Twin Flame and Soul Mates, we have chosen to share with you information that may be pertinent and useful in this regard. Indeed, beloved ones, such beings do exist, but contrary to what you may currently comprehend, not all such beings may be in human form with you when you choose to walk upon the Earth. In the preceding chapter, you were introduced to the concept of disembodied beings of Light. Many of these beings are Twin Flames and Soul Mates. This may be confusing upon first reading, for you may have been led to believe that you have only one soul mate, who is here upon the Earth plane, eagerly awaiting connection with you. And the concept of Twin Flame may be completely new. So let us explain.

TWIN FLAME

Your Twin Flame is a portion of your being that separated from you when you first chose to incarnate into the human plane. Prior to your initial incarnation, you were in your Totality, whole and one. When you chose incarnation, you also chose whether your essence in human form would reflect what can be described as *yin* (female, receptive) or *yang* (masculine, aggressive) energy. These concepts were introduced into the human plane for many reasons which we will not delineate at this time. The primary human function, however, was for the propagation of the species. And so, after you chose either *yin* or *yang*, the part of you that separated and took the other energetic expression would be called, for lack of a better term, your "Twin Flame."[1] No matter what you would choose to call it, there is only one other essence that would comprise the directly opposite portion of your Totality.

We ask you to note well, however, that even though, when you first embodied, you may have initially chosen a certain sexual identity, since that time, through many, many lifetimes, you have also chosen to embody as the opposite sex. And so, in any particular embodiment, you may be female when initially you were male, and your Twin Flame may also be female. Or you may be male, as you were initially, but the *yin* part of your Totality may also have chosen a male embodiment. Or, your Twin Flame may not have chosen embodiment at all in this lifetime, and may be available only from higher vibrational frequencies as you walk the Earth plane.

You may ask if it is important to know your Twin Flame. If it is your heart's desire to make such a conscious connection in this embodiment, and if it is for your Highest Good, then you will choose to do so. You may not choose to have such a conscious connection in every embodiment. Nonetheless, on some level of awareness, as with all and everything, **you are always connected**.

It is well to understand that this portion of your Totality, as with all your Totality, has the potential to be a nurturing energy, once you have gained awareness of it and understand how it is connected to you. It, too, comes from

---

[1] We offer this term for your benefit. You may choose another name for this energy, if you wish, as you may for all that has been described in this manuscript.

Infinite Source, just as you do, and it has experienced many, many embodiments. Your Twin Flame is the sum total of all it has experienced so far, just as you are. And when accessed through its Higher Self, it has great wisdom to share, just as you do.[1]

By opening your heart while you are in a meditative state and surrounded by a healing radiance, you can request a direct connection with your Twin Flame. But be aware, beloved ones, your Twin Flame has been human, or is presently in a human incarnation. If, at this time in its existence, your Twin Flame has not awakened to the point where it is utilizing the Light for its Highest Good you may only gain awareness of its suffering. This is why we suggest that you not attempt this contact prior to reading the chapter on Higher Self.

If you focus your awareness solely on the Higher Self of this inextricable part of you, much healing can take place for both of you. Indeed, all that you are is connected to all that is your Twin Flame, and when one portion of you chooses to consciously address the Light of the other, this can be wondrous and healing for you both. You will have chosen to call forth and recognize the highest vibration of awareness that you both are. That will certainly enhance and heal both of you, for what you honor in another, you will honor in yourself. This is true in all relationships, but it is most emphatically true in regard to one's Twin Flame.

It matters little where your Twin Flame resides at this time. What does matter for you, however, is how you choose

---

[1] In the following chapter we will expand on the topic of the Higher Self. Perhaps it may be useful to understand such more thoroughly before contemplating a connection with your Twin Flame, either on the Earth plane, or in a higher vibrational frequency.

to approach this connection. Be aware of your motives. If you seek your Twin Flame because you believe this will assuage a sense of loneliness, or will allow you to feel more complete regarding self, we tell you that you may be quite disappointed with the results. Your Twin Flame is indeed the other half of your Totality. But you cannot look to it to complete who you are. This can only be accomplished by opening to your own Higher Self, through direct connection to the Light of All and everything. Nothing outside yourself can accomplish such completion for you.

However, connection with your Twin Flame can allow more healing of the scars of life to flow between you, and this can be most useful. When requesting any connection to the Light, remember that all that has been created in this regard has one reason to exist: To help you to heal, and to awaken you to the true nature of your being. The truth of your nature is that **you are light, whole and complete unto yourself**.

SOUL MATES

Soul Mates are beings who have been with you during more than one embodiment, and with whom you have shared many profound experiences that have established a strong karmic bond between you. These are beings who, if they have been in human form with you in this lifetime, will have been your mother, father, brother, sister, mate, child, friend or acquaintance.

You may not know when you will encounter a soul mate, if you are only using your conscious mind to comprehend. In fact, anyone can be a soul mate. You would need to explore your inner awareness (again, this is accomplished most easily in a meditative state) when evaluating a relationship, to ascertain whether a certain person is, indeed, a soul mate. We will say, however, that if the person in question is a parent, child, close family member, or one with whom you have shared sexual intimacy, then in these cases, he or she most definitely is a soul mate.

In instances other than those mentioned above, you may meet someone for the first time and have an experience that might be described as "instant recognition." By that, we mean that you have a feeling that you already "know" this person, even though you have just met for the first time in this lifetime. You may also feel such a profound desire to reconnect with them, that even though it does not make sense to your conscious awareness, you feel compelled to act upon it in any event. Ultimately, you will find yourself in the company of this person more frequently, and much will be shared between you.

These are the humans with whom you have made agreements, before embodiment, to walk down a portion of life's path together, to help one another grow and awaken through shared life experiences. With all soul mates, you will choose to balance karma with one another once again, and in so doing, offer each other life lessons that will be growth opportunities for both.

As you enter the Earth plane, and encounters your soul mates once again, much emotion and feeling will rise, as they have in previous embodiments. In these emotions and feelings lie the seeds from which may come growth towards awakening -- if you choose to step back and observe the dynamic that has brought you together once again.

We recommend that you contact the Higher Self of your soul mate while you are in a meditative state. Ask to be made aware of the nature of your karmic agreement and the lessons you are choosing to learn from your encounters with this person during this lifetime. Much wisdom can be gained from becoming aware of this information. Let us give you an example.

You are born to parents who will nurture and love you to the best of their ability. However, in most instances, human beings will choose parents with whom, in their human awareness, they will be dissatisfied. This dynamic is most prevalent on the Earth plane at this time. Indeed, it is ingrained in the process of human development. Your childhood cannot ever be a completely satisfactory experience for you because, as you are a unique creation, no one upon the human plane can meet all your many needs completely. It is simply impossible. Only a conscious, awakened awareness of your connection to Infinite Source would satisfy your deepest needs, but in your youth, you are not likely to be aware of this.

Your parents, however, will greatly desire a relationship with you that will be satisfying for all parties, where you will feel safe and completely nurtured, and happy with them as parents. Indeed, in their eyes you will appear to be a creation of theirs, and they will place much ego investment in you. And so, while a situation exists where they can never totally satisfy all your needs, in most cases, they will try.

As Leia would say, this is a "set-up." Indeed, she would say all of life is a "set-up." We will not argue with her in the use of this expression. However, we reiterate that all parties choose to create these "set-ups" in their karmic agreements with their soul mates.[1] The "set-up" in the relationship with your parents would be designed to balance many karmic issues while you are experiencing the stresses

---

[1] This would also be true in regard to your Twin Flame.

and strains of this relationship. You would also have an opportunity to become aware of your innate desire to awaken to the Light within, and to use this experience to heal yourself and your relationship with these soul mates who agreed to be your parents.

Now, how does one realize such desire for oneself? The answer, again, is to sit quietly in a safe space of healing Light and request connection to the Higher Self of each other being involved. This connection to the Higher Self of another can be accomplished whether or not the being is in human form at this time. We would also encourage you to invoke the healing radiance of other beings of Light (such as Angels, Archangels or Masters) to aid you in this process. For you see, beloved ones, when you choose such a connection, it may be a time when much emotion and feeling will arise in you that you may wish to heal. These beings of Light can be quite useful to you for this purpose. All you need do is ask, and they will be with you.

You can learn much from pursuing this connection. Soul Mates (and Twin Flames) are one's greatest teachers while one resides upon the human plane. They have agreed to be your catalysts to awakening in this embodiment, as you have chosen to be their catalysts in the same process. Once you become aware of this fact, forgiveness, unconditional love, acceptance and ultimately awakening can be the result. Be patient, kind, loving, and compassionate to self as you endeavor to comprehend the significance of these teachers.

As with Twin Flames, not all soul mates will be embodied with you at any given time. If a being comes to you from another vibrational frequency, as described in the preceding chapter regarding disembodied beings and "Guardian Angels," this most often is a soul mate who is seeking to establish or maintain a connection with you. This being may have been a family member, former mate, or close companion who has made their transition back into the realm of spirit. As previously described, you may choose to allow an active connection or not, depending upon whether it is in your Highest Good at this time. This decision is solely within your power.

Unlike Angels, Archangels, and Ascended Masters, who do honor your free will, these beings will come unbidden. Your soul mates or Twin Flame may desire to complete some of their karma through you, as you still reside upon the human plane. You will not be judged if you do not choose to cooperate. If the being might benefit more from staying within the healing radiance of the Light rather than with you, by all means offer the opportunity by invoking a column of Light to enfold the being, and send the being to the Light.

In any event, it is within your power to insist that this being not remain with you, if you do not wish it. Simply invoke the healing radiance of the Light to surround you at all times, and the unwelcome being cannot penetrate such to be with you.

As you heal, and gain awareness of the many blessings that all these beings offer in service of your awakening, you will feel more inclined to have an open, compassionate heart for all of them. Indeed, **you will awaken to the realization that all is One**, and all with whom you have been connected are simply a manifestation of the One, the Infinite Source. Be patient, loving, and compassionate to self, continue to invoke the Light and Beings of Light for your own healing, and ultimately such a realization can come to you.

Chapter 10

Knowing Your Higher Self

Throughout this publication, we have often referred to one's Higher Self. Now it is time to explain this concept in greater depth. *Higher Self* is a term that humanity has been using more frequently in recent times. In this publication we have occasionally used *Totality* or *Entity* as alternative terms for *Higher Self*. Please note these terms may be used interchangeably to describe the same concept. For the sake of simplicity, we shall use *Higher Self*.

However, we find any of these terms limiting, as there are no human words to completely describe the concept we will attempt to convey. We will do what we can, within the limitations imposed by your language, with the understanding that you must go within and comprehend for yourself, and have your own unique experience.

The experiences available to you in connection with the Angels, Archangels, and other beings of Light described so far are simply a means to an end. The "end" we speak of is your desire -- in every fiber of your being -- to comprehend and make use of an experience of your Higher Self, and infuse that consciousness into all that occurs while you are human. That sounds a bit much, doesn't it?

You may say, well, Master, whatever this Higher Self is in relation to me, do I have to wish to comprehend this thing to the point where I would be using that awareness in *everything* I do while I am human? And we will say, *absolutely!* All that we have inspired Leia to write in these publications is simply guidance to lead you to this very point.

Nothing else you ever do as a human can be more important to you.

For many, it is enough to have an awareness that there is Light, and that the Light can be helpful. For many, it is enough to comprehend how one can heal oneself with this Light. It may be enough to comprehend how one can use healing affirmations in creating change within one's life. For others, knowing of the other vibrational frequencies, and the beings of Light that inhabit them, may be satisfactory. Or giving away your power to a Being of Light, and allowing that being to guide you, may satisfy all your desires in this embodiment.

We will tell you that there is still more that can be accomplished, that will indeed create the most profound and healing change within you. All the above awarenesses and experiences are simply aids in achieving comprehension of your own Higher Self -- and then using your realization in all you are doing. Nothing, we repeat, **nothing can compare with realizing this awareness as fully as possible in any lifetime.**

Now, we do not say that this is an easy thing for most humans to do. Indeed not. Most certainly it has not been easy in recent times because of all the distractions that life on the Earth plane has to offer. However, we will say that as the frequency of the Earth plane has increased, **it has become easier to succeed in this endeavor than it has in eons.** So, it is significant that you are interested in learning more about your Higher Self at this time. And for this, we honor you and offer our services to aid you in this process, as do all the beings of Light who are here to support you in knowing your own Higher Self.

Let us endeavor to describe the concept of the Higher Self to you. First, we should reiterate that you will have your own unique experience of such and it is to be honored. We therefore speak in general terms to enable some awareness of your Higher Self that can help you begin to comprehend.

Imagine, to the best of your ability at this time, that you, as a unique Spark of Light, have emanated from the Infinite Source of All and everything. As you gained awareness of all of Creation, you became attracted to one portion more than another. The reasons such an attraction occurred cannot be accurately comprehended with the human mind. Suffice it to say that such an "electromagnetic" attraction did occur, and you found your spark of Light choosing to participate actively in this region of Creation called "the Earth plane." Thus, an emanation or portion of your unique Spark of Light chose to "enter" (for the sake of this description) the Earth plane. Only a portion of you entered the Earth plane. Your direct connection to Infinite Source would always remain intact and inviolate, regardless of any experiences you might have anywhere in Creation.

If this was your first embodiment, the portion of you that entered the Earth plane would have split in two to become either *yin* or *yang* essence, manifesting as female or male. Subsequent embodiments, as we mentioned in the description of Twin Flames, may have been either as male or female for karmic balance. But your initial essence would always remain unchanged, either *yin* or *yang*.

In the course of your embodiments, you assumed many different identities in different lifetimes, and established what would be called karmic patterns. All your experiences attached themselves to your original Spark of Light, allowing an ever-expanding awareness of self through all you experienced in your embodiments. Simultaneously, this Spark of Light has all of the awareness of Infinite

Source. It has a direct and inviolate link to Infinite Source, because it is, indeed, a portion of Infinite Source!

This Spark, with all its awareness and experience of Infinite Source, and with the many experiences it has had in Creation, is what we shall call **Higher Self. It is your direct link to Infinite Source, and it is the sum total of all that you have ever known in any embodiment in any part of Creation at any time and in any space.** It has access to All and everything that has happened anywhere in Creation at any time. Because of this, it comprehends everything.

The human mind cannot do such. It can only truly comprehend that which lies within the awareness and perception available from an Earth plane perspective. This human mind has been a very useful thing to you. It has aided you quite well in your functioning upon the Earth plane. But because the Higher Self holds a simultaneous awareness of the Earth plane, Infinite Source, and all of Creation, it is capable of a wisdom and understanding that the human mind can scarcely imagine.

Indeed, all of humanity, at one time or another, has endeavored to achieve this understanding. As we have stated, all the religions of the world, and the philosophies, arts and sciences as well, have had as their goal this wisdom and understanding of All and everything. Ironically, all this information is already an integral part of each and every being upon the human plane!

It has never been necessary to go anywhere at any time trying to grasp what the human mind cannot grasp by searching outside itself. The only thing that has always been necessary is simply to go within.

In the face of the intoxicating choices that living on Earth offered, and that could not be experienced on other planes of existence, human beings chose to forget their true nature. Instead, they chose to grasp pleasure without wisdom and compassion. Consequently, some humans decided to step in and to regulate such behaviors for the sake of all. It seemed evident that humanity was naturally incapable of handling its affairs responsibly, i.e., with wisdom and compassion. Thus, humanity chose the experiences that led to the creation of religions in order to regulate itself.

Through the course of history, various religions developed which offered some esoteric knowledge of the true nature of human beings. Many of the world's religions decided, however, that wisdom and understanding could only be achieved through the study of particular teachings and writings, presented in the context of a hierarchy that could be regulated by the religious authorities. Furthermore, much effort was expended in creating ways for individuals to prove themselves worthy before they could learn anything of their true nature.

We do not judge religions as right or wrong, as we do not judge anything that has been done anywhere in Creation. At the time that religion was created, it was in perfect order for what humanity chose to need at that time.

This, however, has led humans to believe that they are still unable, or "not good enough," to know the true nature of their being, or to grasp an understanding of All and everything. Having been told for centuries that their natural state is "bad" has led humanity to believe that their lot is to suffer in darkness, a darkness which can only be alleviated by searching outside oneself for something to reduce this suffering. Hence, addictions, greed and fear have become widespread. For if one does not know that one is whole and complete within the Light, then one will choose to look elsewhere for solace.

75

Now that the Earth plane is choosing to awaken rapidly, we will tell you that the time of suffering in darkness is ending. We tell you that what you need to know to awaken to your true nature is within you *now*. It always has been. We tell you that you already are a being of Light within a human form. This Light you may call your Higher Self. And we tell you that you can access this Higher Self on your own, in your own times of meditative peace and quiet.

However, we also tell you that opening to your Higher Self is not to be done solely with your mind. You *must* open your heart to allow awareness of this Light to fill your being. This wisdom, this awareness will come through your heart, not through your mind. **The heart is the center** and the main conduit for this Light of Higher Self to pour into your form.[1] As you allow yourself to breathe this Light into your heart, you awaken and you know.

Then, as you sit quietly, you may enlist the aid of any of the Angels, Archangels, or beings of Light to help you with this process. Do not be afraid, dear ones. You can do this thing. You have nothing to lose but the darkness within. Realize the Light that has always been who you are. This Light can show you your true nature. There will not be words to describe this. You will have an intrinsic understanding that will change all that you perceive. A clarity and peace will come to you as you allow an awareness of this Light to fill you.

Be patient with the process as it unfolds and shows itself to you. Nothing at all is required by the human mind after you have consciously requested that you wish an

---

[1] See *Balancing the Light Within* for information regarding the Chakra system.

awakening to your Higher Self.[1] And so, as you allow the human thoughts to rest, and simply request the heart to open to your Higher Self, you will experience a surrender, a letting go. As you let go, trust that this Light of Higher Self, which is your true nature, can guide you with greater wisdom than your mind has ever known. We do not say this is easy. That is why we are here to help you. That is why we ask you to trust, surrender and be patient with the process.

Once you open yourself to wanting the experience, it will happen. The Light of your Higher Self will aid you in shedding all the misunderstandings and illusions that life upon the Earth plane has left within you for all these many centuries. You will experience a freedom that comes with understanding that all you have ever desired or wanted has always been within you. Grasp it and know it to be your own truth that can guide you with a wisdom heretofore unknown to your human mind.

We offer you great blessings of Love and Light as you proceed upon your journey to the beginning and the end. To Alpha and Omega. To All and everything. **We are with you always.**

---

[1] See *Affirmations and Thought Forms* for specific affirmations.

77

Appendix A

Suggested Readings

The following is a collection of titles we have found useful and informative in our studies of metaphysics in the wider sense. The list is far from comprehensive and there are many other equally valuable publications. We include these suggested readings as a service to those who might wish to deepen their understanding of some of the topics touched upon in this book.

If you do enter a bookstore or library, we suggest that you quiet your mind and try to listen to the "still, small voice within" as you are holding a book which has caught your interest. If you feel a "resonance" with this book, it is likely that this is a useful step on your path to greater awareness; if it does not "speak" to you, no matter how much others may have recommended it, find another book to take home. Relying on guidance from your Higher Self, and honoring your own truth, is always the wisest course of action.

General Reading
- *The Dreaming Universe* and *Parallel Universes,* by Fred Alan Wolf
- *The Holographic Universe,* by Michael Talbot
- *Saint Germain on Alchemy: Formulas for Self-Transformation*, by M. Prophet & E. Clare Prophet
- *Phaedrus* and *Symposium*, by Plato
- *Bhagavad-Gita: The Song of God,* translated by Swami Prabhavananda & Christopher Isherwood (or others)
- *The Upanishads,* translated by Prabhavananda

- *Yoga,* by Vivekananda
- *Autobiography of a Yogi,* by Paramahansa Yogananda
- *Hidden Journey,* by Andrew Harvey (on Mother Meera)
- *Tao Te Ching*
- *The Tibetan Book of Living and Dying,* by Sogyal Rinpoche
- *Seth Speaks,* by Jane Roberts
- *Channeling: Investigation on Receiving Information from Paranormal Sources,* by John Klimo
- *There is a River: A Biography of Edgar Cayce,* by Thomas Sugrue
- *River of Compassion,* by Bede Griffiths
- *The Kyrian Letters,* by Sandra Redhoff
- *A Child of Eternity,* by Adriana Rocha & Kristi Jorde
- *Conversations with God: An Uncommon Dialogue,* by Neale Donald Walsch
- *The Hathor Material: Messages from an Ascended Civilization,* by Tom Kenyon and Virginia Essene
- *Emissary of Light: My Adventures With the Secret Peacemakers,* by James F. Twyman
- *Angels and Other Beings of Light: They are Here to Help You! A Discourse from the Ascended Master St. Germain*, by Linda Stein-Luthke and Martin F. Luthke

Earth Changes
- *Mary's Message to the World,* by Annie Kirkwood
- *Kryon: The End Times (New information for personal peace),* Kryon channeled by Lee Carroll
- *World Evolution: Our Future in the 21st Century,* by Margaret McCormick
- *Awakening to Zero Point: The Collective Initiation,* by Gregg Braden

- *Earth Changes Report: Preparing for the New Millennium,* and *Future Map of North America*, by Gordon-Michael Scallion (800-628-7493)
- *I Am America Map* and *Freedom Star World Map,* by Lori Adaile Toye (800-930-1341)
- *Riding the Tide of Change: Preparing for Personal & Planetary Transformation,* by Martin F. Luthke

Reincarnation
- *Return from Tomorrow,* by George G. Ritchie with Elizabeth Sherrill
- *Life After Life* and *The Light Beyond,* by Raymond A. Moody
- *Closer to the Light,* by Melvin Morse with Paul Perry
- *Many Lives, Many Masters,* by Brian L. Weiss
- *Embraced by the Light,* by Betty J. Eadie
- *Reincarnation and Immortality,* by Rudolph Steiner
- *Reincarnation,* by Helen Wambaugh
- *Talking to Heaven,* by James van Praagh

Healing, Chakras and Auras
- *The Healer's Manual: A Beginner's Guide to Vibrational Therapies,* by Ted Andrews
- *How to See & Read the Aura,* by Ted Andrews
- *Man Visible and Invisible* and *The Chakras,* by C.W. Leadbeater
- *You Can Heal Your Life,* by Louise Hay
- *Quantum Healing,* and other books by Deepak Chopra
- *Hands of Light: A Guide to Healing Through the Human Energy Field,* by Barbara A. Brennan
- *Balancing the Light Within: A Discourse on Healing from the Ascended Master St. Germain,* by Linda Stein-Luthke and Martin F. Luthke

Appendix B

Books by the Authors

Expansion Publishing is offering the following titles by Linda Stein-Luthke and Martin F. Luthke, Ph.D.:

• **Balancing the Light Within.** *A Discourse on Healing from the Ascended Master St. Germain,* by Linda Stein-Luthke and Martin F. Luthke, ISBN 0-9656927-0-1, 54 pp., US $6.95. A channeled discourse on light vibrations, tools of awareness, chakras, healing of self and others with metaphysical means; suggested readings.

• **Affirmations and Thought Forms: You Can Change Your Mind!** *A Discourse from the Ascended Master St. Germain,* by Linda Stein-Luthke and Martin F. Luthke, ISBN 0-9656927-1-X, 48 pp., US $6.95. A channeled discourse on the use of affirmations and the power of thought forms and how to use both for healing purposes, with an emphasis on self-empowerment and self-awareness; suggested readings.

• **Angels and Other Beings of Light: They are Here to Help You!** *A Discourse from the Ascended Master St. Germain,* by Linda Stein-Luthke and Martin F. Luthke, ISBN 0-9656927-3-6, 84 pp., US $8.95. A channeled discourse on working with angels, Archangels, Ascended Masters, twin flame, soul mates, and other beings of Light; who they are; what their purpose is; how to contact them; how to experience your Higher Self; suggested readings.

81

- ***Riding the Tide of Change: Preparing for Personal & Planetary Transformation***, by Martin F. Luthke, ISBN 0-9656927-2-8, 108 pp., US $9.95. A metaphysical book on Earth changes with an emphasis on releasing fears, healing self, and understanding our role as co-creators during this time of transformation; suggested readings.

- ***Beyond Psychotherapy: Introduction to Psychoenergetic Healing***, by Martin F. Luthke and Linda Stein-Luthke, ISBN 0-9656927-4-4, 228 pp., US $19.95. This book by the founders of Psychoenergetic Healing describes an advanced approach to the healing of emotional, mental, spiritual and physical issues. A groundbreaking introduction for healers, psychotherapists, and all who are interested in energy-based healing methods.

- ***Navigating the Fourth Dimension:*** *A Discourse from the Ascended Masters St. Germain and El Morya Khan,* by Linda Stein-Luthke and Martin F. Luthke, ISBN 0-9656927-5-2, 134 pp., US $11.95. A channeled discourse explaining why the past no longer applies and proposing new ways of thinking, being, and creating that can lead to an experience of harmony, balance, peace, and abundance in the here and now. The appendix contains the first ten issues of the *Ascended Masters Newsletter*.

- ***Dispelling the Illusions of Aging and Dying:*** *A Discourse from the Ascended Masters St. Germain,* by Linda Stein-Luthke and Martin F. Luthke, ISBN 0-9656927-6-0, 90 pp., US $11.95. The two greatest fears that human beings possess are the fears of aging and dying. If you follow the suggestions offered by the *Ascended Master St. Germain* and heal your fears, you will move into a greater awareness of the only true reality there is: that *all is Light* -- and that includes you. The appendix contains seven issues of the *Ascended Masters Newsletter*.

Free Newsletter

We invite you to subscribe to the *Ascended Masters Newsletter*. This electronic publication offers channeled wisdom from the Ascended Masters as well as information about new books, workshops, and training opportunities. To subscribe, please send a blank e-mail to newsletter-subscribe@u-r-light.com. Past editions of the newsletter can be found on our website ***www.u-r-light.com*** under "Archives."

How to Order Books

• **On-line orders**: For more information, excerpts, and secure on-line orders please visit *www.u-r-light.com*. Credit cards and Paypal accepted. You may e-mail any inquiries to *expansion@u-r-light.com*. Please contact us for resale or quantity discounts.

• **Mail-in orders**: Please send your order -- including your e-mail address, if available -- to: Expansion Publishing, P.O. Box 516, Chagrin Falls, OH 44022, USA. We gladly accept credit cards (with name, number, expiration date), US-checks, or money orders.

• **Shipping for domestic orders**: Please add $2.00 for orders totaling up to $10, $3.00 for orders between $10 and $20, and $4.00 for orders over $20.

• **Shipping for international orders**: Please add $4.00 for orders totaling up to $10; $5.00 for orders between $10 and $20; and $6.00 for orders over $20.

• **Bookstores**: All titles are also available through your local bookstore. However, you may need to special-order them.

• **Phone orders**: Please call **Expansion Publishing** (888-240-2822) for credit card orders.